CONTENTS

KU-468-519

INTRODUCTION

Changing views

Long ago, people believed that feelings and emotions came from different parts of the body. They thought that bravery and love were based in the heart, with fear in the stomach and anger in the liver. Today we know that all these emotions and feelings happen in the brain. The brain is also the site of all our ideas, wishes, wants and memories – in fact, everything to do with thinking. It is the site of what we call 'the mind'.

MESSAGES IN

Like a supercomputer in the middle of a vast computer network, the brain is the control centre for the body. It receives millions of messages every second, carrying information about what is happening outside the body, detected by the eyes, ears and other senses. The brain also monitors conditions inside the body, such as the heart's beating, digestion in the stomach, and the body's temperature.

We cannot see the brain working. But we can see when people are deep in thought and concentration, from their facial expressions and precise actions.

OUR BODIES

THE BRAIN AND NERVOUS SYSTEM

Steve Parker

ONE WEEK LOAN

HODDER
Wayland

an imprint of Hodder Children's Books

Titles in the series:
The Brain and Nervous System • Digestion
The Heart, Lungs and Blood • Reproduction
The Senses • The Skeleton and Muscles

For more information on this series and other Hodder Wayland titles, go www.hodderwayland.co.uk

Produced by Monkey Puzzle Media Ltd
Gissing's Farm, Fressingfield, Suffolk IP21 5SH, UK

Text copyright © 2003 Steve Parker
Series copyright © 2003 Hodder Wayland
First published in 2003 by Hodder Wayland
an imprint of Hodder Children's Books
This paperback edition published in 2006

Commissioning Editor: Victoria Brooker
Book Editor: Nicola Edwards
Design: Jane Hawkins
Picture Research: Sally Cole
Artwork: Peter Bull
Consultant: Dr Trish Groves

British Library Cataloguing in Publication Data
Parker, Steve, 1952-
  The brain and nervous system. – (Our bodies)
  1. Brain – Juvenile literature 2. Nervous system - Juvenile literature
  I. Title
  612.8'2

ISBN 07502 3722 8

Printed and bound in China

Hodder Children's Books
A division of Hodder Headline Limited
338 Euston Road, London NW1 3BH

Picture Acknowledgements
Ardea 9 top (Hayden Oake); Corbis 4 (LWA-JDC), 38 (David Turnley); Corbis Digital Stock 29 bottom; Digital Vision 1, 13 top, 20 bottom, 33, 41; FLPA 7 (Tony Wharton), 37 (Martin B. Withers); Getty Images 36 (Taxi); ImageState *front cover* main image, 5; Robert Harding Picture Library 19 top (Sharp Shooters); Science Photo Library *front cover* inset (Catherine Pouedras/ Eurelios), 11 bottom (Tek Image), 13 bottom (Samuel Ashfield), 15 top (BSIP, James Cavallini), 15 bottom (Volker Steger), 17 (Dr John Zajicek), 23 (Mehau Kulyk), 24 (Steve Grand), 26 (TRL Ltd), 27 (GCa-CNRI), 31 (Catherine Pouedras/Eurelios), 35 (Innerspace Imaging), 43 (Simon Fraser), 45 (BSIP, Laurent/Lae. Hop Amer); Topham Picturepoint/ImageWorks 16, 21 bottom, 29 top, 42.

In high-speed action, like skiing, the brain makes many decisions every second, to control muscles and movements.

MESSAGES OUT

Using this vast amount of incoming information, the brain sends out messages to regulate and alter hundreds of body parts and processes. Again, this happens at the rate of millions of messages every second. In this way, the brain makes sure that all parts of the body work together in a coordinated way. In particular, the brain controls the muscles which make the body move.

LINKS TO THE BODY

Messages to and from the brain travel along nerves. These are like the bundles of electrical wires and optical fibres used for computer networks and the Internet. The messages themselves are in the form of tiny pulses or bursts of electricity, called nerve impulses or nerve signals. The nerve network spreads out through the body, sending branches to every part, carrying information to and fro. Together, the brain and all of the nerves are known as the body's nervous system.

PARTS OF THE NERVOUS SYSTEM

A multi-part system

The body's nervous system is really three systems in one. First is the brain itself, and its main link with the body, the spinal cord, which passes down inside the back. These two parts make up the central nervous system. Second is the network of nerves that branch out from the brain and spinal cord, and spread into all parts of the body. This network is known as the peripheral nervous system. ('Peripheral' means 'away from the centre' or 'towards the outside'.)

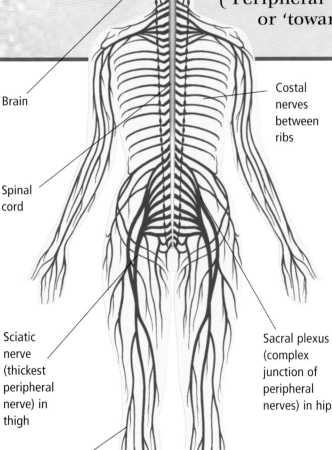

Brain

Spinal cord

Costal nerves between ribs

Sciatic nerve (thickest peripheral nerve) in thigh

Sacral plexus (complex junction of peripheral nerves) in hip

Peroneal nerve in calf

RUNNING ON 'AUTO'

Third is the autonomic nervous system. This works like the body's 'autopilot'. It continually checks and monitors what is happening inside the body, and makes alterations and adjustments, to keep conditions inside the body constant, and to control vital bodily processes like breathing and heart rate. It is described on pages 20–21.

The nervous system's main structural parts are the brain and spinal cord of the central nervous system, and the bodywide network of peripheral nerves (in green).

weblinks

To find out more about the nervous system, go to:
www.waylinks.co.uk/series/ourbodies/brainandnervous

PROTECTING THE SYSTEM

The brain is soft and delicate. It is well protected inside the dome-shaped part of the skull called the cranium. This is made of hard bone and shields the brain from knocks and bumps. The spinal cord is also well protected from knocks, twists and kinks. It is in a tunnel within the row of bones called vertebrae which make up the spine (spinal column or backbone).

Try this!

Tap your head gently. (Hopefully it does not sound hollow.) Hear and feel the hard skull bone just under the skin. This is the body's own 'hard-hat' to protect the delicate brain inside.

ANIMAL VERSUS HUMAN

A starfish does not have a proper brain. It has a ring of nerves around its central part, where the arms join together. Starfish are amazingly numerous, swarming in their millions in every ocean. So big brains are not essential for success.

The starfish lacks a brain, as does the jellyfish, yet both creatures are very numerous.

The main nerve

The spinal cord is the link between body and brain. It is about 45 centimetres long and as wide as a little finger. It is housed in a tunnel within the vertebrae, or backbones, of the spinal column. The spinal cord's upper end merges with the base of the brain. Its lower end, at about waist level, branches into separate nerves which run down the remainder of the spinal column.

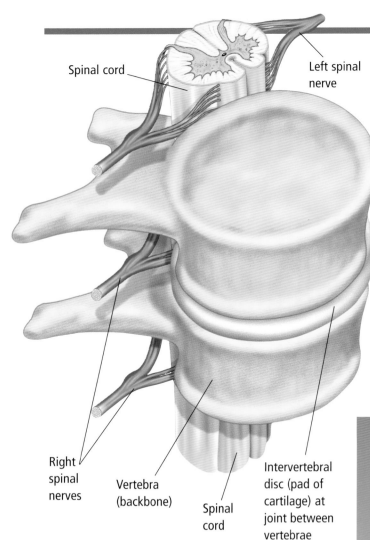

Spinal cord

Left spinal nerve

Right spinal nerves

Vertebra (backbone)

Spinal cord

Intervertebral disc (pad of cartilage) at joint between vertebrae

The spinal cord is inside a tunnel within the spinal column. The spinal nerves join to it at the gaps between the vertebrae (backbones), where the bones are held apart slightly by cushion-like discs.

SPINAL NERVES

There are 31 pairs of spinal nerves that join to the spinal cord, on the left and right sides. The spinal nerves branch from the cord at gaps in the joints between the vertebrae (backbones), and spread out into the body. The uppermost nerves, in the neck, extend down the arms and hands. The middle ones send branches to the chest and abdomen. The lowest spinal nerves extend into the legs. All of these nerves carry signals to and fro, between body parts and the spinal cord.

Top Tips

The upper spinal cord is at risk when a vehicle stops suddenly in an accident and jerks the neck with great force, a movement called 'whiplash'. This can cause pain and even paralysis (inability to move) of parts of the body below the neck, although whiplash is rarely fatal. A seatbelt and a properly adjusted headrest help greatly to lessen whiplash and any resulting neck injury.

INSIDE THE SPINAL CORD

A slice through the cord would show an H-shaped darker area of grey matter, set within a paler area of white matter. The white matter is mainly nerve fibres, carrying nerve signals up and down the cord, and linking to the brain. The grey matter is largely the cell bodies of nerve cells, with their millions of dendrites (see page 11) connecting to each other.

The spinal cord contains areas of white matter (here shown pinkish) surrounding grey matter (shown here in light green). Each spinal nerve divides into two roots, which then split into smaller rootlets as they join the cord.

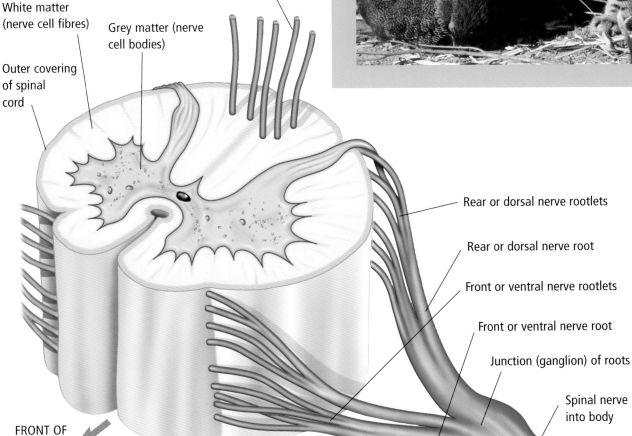

Nerve fibres running up and down cord

White matter
(nerve cell fibres)

Grey matter (nerve
cell bodies)

Outer covering
of spinal
cord

FRONT OF
BODY

Rear or dorsal nerve rootlets

Rear or dorsal nerve root

Front or ventral nerve rootlets

Front or ventral nerve root

Junction (ganglion) of roots

Spinal nerve
into body

ANIMAL VERSUS HUMAN

An expert predator like the wild cat pounces on a victim and immediately bites the back of its neck hard. This cuts or breaks the prey's spinal cord, so it cannot move and soon dies.

Predators such as cats, wolves, stoats and birds of prey often attack the prey's neck to damage the spinal cord.

NERVE CELLS

Different shapes and sizes

Like all living things, the human body is made of billions and billions of tiny cells, of many different kinds. Most can only be seen under a microscope – about 20,000 of them would fit inside this 'o'. The cells of the nervous system differ from most other body cells in several ways – especially in their shape and size, and in how they are linked to each other.

A typical nerve cell has many short branches, dendrites, and one main longer, thicker one, the axon or fibre.

Axon (fibre)

Myelin sheath around axon

Dendrites

Nerve cell nucleus (control centre)

Nerve cell body

Dendrites

Axon terminals (endings)

THE NERVE CELL

The main types of cells in the nervous system are nerve cells or neurons. There are many billions in the brain alone. The main part, or cell body, of a nerve cell is similar in size and shape to the cell bodies of other cells. It has the usual parts, including its own control centre or nucleus.

Top Tips

In some sports and activities there is a risk of injury which might trap or pinch a nerve, especially where it passes near a joint. This can cause pain, numbness and inability to move the body part. Protective joint guards, such as elbow shields and knee pads, help to reduce the risk.

DENDRITES

A nerve cell differs from other cells in two main ways – its dendrites and its axon (fibre). Dendrites are thin, spidery branches from the main cell body. They spread out and link to other nerve cells nearby, and receive nerve signals from them. A single nerve cell may have tens of thousands of dendrites, receiving signals from thousands of other nerve cells.

AXONS

A nerve cell also has a longer and thicker part, called the axon or nerve fibre. In many nerves this axon is covered by a layer of fatty substance, known as a myelin sheath. At its end, the axon links to other nerve cells (or muscles). It passes nerve signals to them, rather than receiving signals from them. Some nerve cells have axons almost one metre in length, making them by far the longest cells in the whole body, although a single axon is far too thin to see.

BIPOLAR NERVE CELL
(cell body part way along axon)

UNIPOLAR NERVE CELL
(cell body on side branch of axon)

Dendrites

Cell body

Axon (fibre)

Axon terminals

MULTIPOLAR NERVE CELL
(cell body at one end of axon)

There are many different nerve cell shapes, which pass on their nerve messages in differing ways.

Nerve cells are especially delicate and easily damaged by poisonous chemicals – and the damage may be permanent. Industrial workers take many precautions against touching or breathing in possibly harmful chemicals.

The nerve impulse

A nerve cell is specialized to receive and send messages, in the form of nerve impulses or signals. A single impulse is like a tiny surge of electricity. It is received from another nerve cell by a dendrite. The impulse travels across the cell body and away along the axon, to be sent on to the dendrites of other nerve cells.

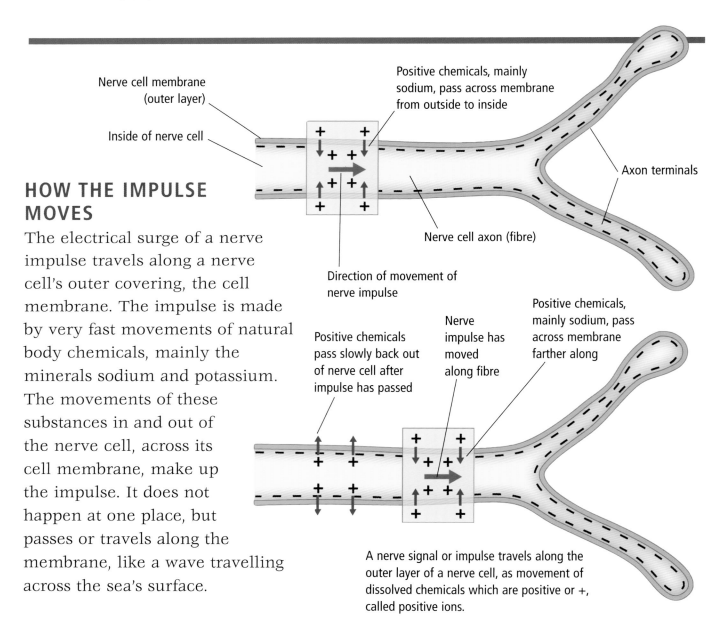

Nerve cell membrane (outer layer)

Inside of nerve cell

Positive chemicals, mainly sodium, pass across membrane from outside to inside

Axon terminals

HOW THE IMPULSE MOVES

Nerve cell axon (fibre)

Direction of movement of nerve impulse

The electrical surge of a nerve impulse travels along a nerve cell's outer covering, the cell membrane. The impulse is made by very fast movements of natural body chemicals, mainly the minerals sodium and potassium. The movements of these substances in and out of the nerve cell, across its cell membrane, make up the impulse. It does not happen at one place, but passes or travels along the membrane, like a wave travelling across the sea's surface.

Positive chemicals pass slowly back out of nerve cell after impulse has passed

Nerve impulse has moved along fibre

Positive chemicals, mainly sodium, pass across membrane farther along

A nerve signal or impulse travels along the outer layer of a nerve cell, as movement of dissolved chemicals which are positive or +, called positive ions.

JUMPING THE GAP

Where the axon of one nerve cell links to the dendrites of another, these parts do not actually touch. There are tiny gaps between them, called synaptic gaps. A synaptic gap is about one hundred times narrower than a human hair. Even so, this is too wide for nerve impulses to 'jump' across, like a spark leaping across a gap between two electrical contacts. Instead, the signal passes across the gap in the form of hundreds of particles of specialized chemicals, called neurotransmitters. These touch the receiving nerve cell and cause the nerve impulse to begin again.

ANIMAL VERSUS HUMAN

When snakes like cobras and mambas bite, they release poison that contains chemical substances called neurotoxins. These damage the nervous system, usually by stopping neurotransmitter chemicals from passing signals between nerve cells. Nerves cannot carry signals to the muscles for movement or to the lungs for breathing. So the snake's victim is paralyzed (unable to move) and may die of suffocation.

The cobra's bite jabs a neurotoxic venom into the body, which spreads and affects vital nerves within minutes.

Sometimes it can help to stop nerve signals travelling to the brain. An anaesthetic does this to remove feelings, especially pain. A local anaesthetic does this for only part of the body, such as the teeth and gums when visiting the dentist.

On the outside

Nerves have a tough, protective, grey outer layer or sheath called the epineurium, made of a substance called myelin. The body's thickest nerve, as wide as a thumb, is the sciatic nerve in the hip and upper leg. The thinnest nerves are in the muscles and are almost too narrow to see.

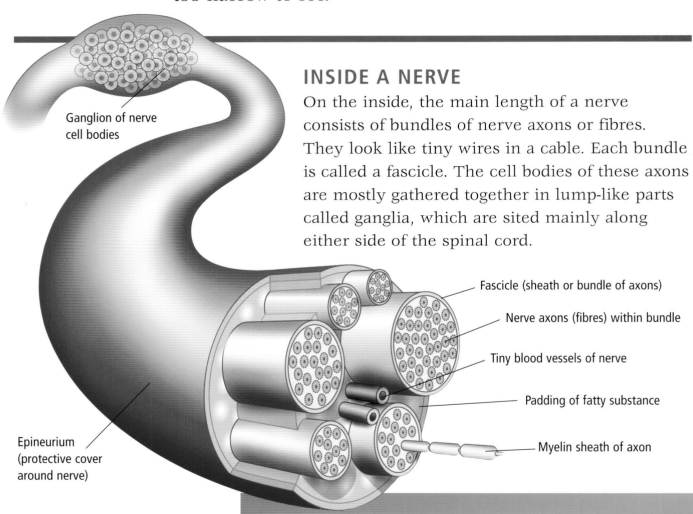

Ganglion of nerve cell bodies

INSIDE A NERVE

On the inside, the main length of a nerve consists of bundles of nerve axons or fibres. They look like tiny wires in a cable. Each bundle is called a fascicle. The cell bodies of these axons are mostly gathered together in lump-like parts called ganglia, which are sited mainly along either side of the spinal cord.

Fascicle (sheath or bundle of axons)

Nerve axons (fibres) within bundle

Tiny blood vessels of nerve

Padding of fatty substance

Myelin sheath of axon

Epineurium (protective cover around nerve)

A nerve is like an electrical multi-core cable, with many nerve fibres wrapped as bundles, along with a blood supply. Fatty padding cushions these parts as the nerve bends with body movements.

Try this!

Do you know of a computer connected to many pieces of equipment, like a keyboard, mouse, camera, scanner, microphone, monitor screen, printer and loudspeaker? Imagine the computer itself as a brain. Which pieces of equipment are 'sensory', sending signals to the computer, and which are 'motor', receiving messages from it? In this system, what are the 'nerves'?

SIGNALS THROUGH THE SYSTEM

A single nerve impulse has a strength of about one-tenth of one volt. (A typical torch battery is 15 times stronger.) The impulse is also very brief, lasting about one millisecond (one-thousandth of a second). Millions of nerve impulses pass around the nervous system every second, and all are much the same. The information they carry depends on how many signals there are per second, and where they are going. Some go to the brain, carrying information from a sense organ like the eye. These are known as sensory signals. Other messages go from the brain, and most – called motor signals – mainly go to muscles to control the body's movements.

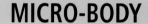

A scan of the inside of the upper leg shows how nerves like the sciatic nerve (arrowed) must withstand squashing by powerful muscles around them.

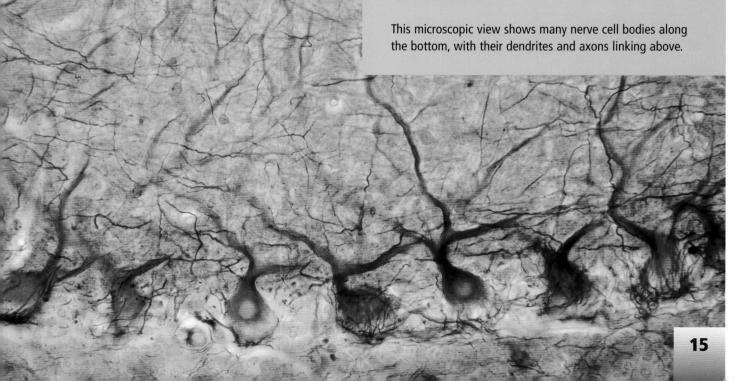

MICRO-BODY

Under a microscope, the nerve network looks impossibly tangled. However the individual nerve cells have very precise and accurate connections with each other.

This microscopic view shows many nerve cell bodies along the bottom, with their dendrites and axons linking above.

NERVE DISORDERS

Nerve symptoms

When the body's peripheral nerves are affected, this can cause serious problems in the parts of the body they supply. These problems include numbness (inability to feel touches), weakness and trembling, spasm (uncontrolled tightening or contraction of muscles), paralysis (inability to move), and perhaps pain from the nerve itself.

CHEMICAL DAMAGE

Some chemical substances are very harmful to nerve cells. They include various drugs used in non-medical ways, especially narcotic drugs such as morphine and heroin, which interfere with the way nerve signals pass from one nerve cell to the next. Other harmful substances include the drug alcohol, metallic chemicals like mercury, lead and cadmium, and poisons in certain plants, and fungi like mushrooms. Nerve cells are especially sensitive to such chemical damage. Also, many body cells can repair or replace themselves. But nerve cells are so specialized, this rarely happens. So any damage they suffer is very long-lasting.

One way of obtaining tiny natural particles of gold from water, is by combining them with the silvery liquid metal, mercury. But mercury is very dangerous and causes great damage to the nervous system.

MULTIPLE SCLEROSIS

In multiple sclerosis, the myelin sheaths around nerve fibres break down. The fibres cannot carry nerve signals properly. This may happen in several nerves, for example, those from the eyes, affecting sight, and those to various muscles, causing weakness. Usually the condition comes and goes over many years. Many people with the condition have no or little permanent disability. A few suffer greater problems, such as needing a wheelchair for mobility.

MOTOR NEURON DISEASE

Motor neuron disease affects nerve cells which carry signals to muscles. This interferes with movements, including speech, chewing and swallowing, and even breathing. The muscles gradually become weak and wasted. As with multiple sclerosis, there is no known cure.

MICROBE ATTACK

In shingles, germs called *Herpes zoster* viruses multiply and attack certain nerves. This causes intense, burning pain in the nerve, and usually blisters on the skin above the nerve. The *Herpes zoster* virus also causes chickenpox, and shingles tends to occur in people who have had chickenpox in the past.

MICRO-BODY

Myelin sheaths work like the plastic insulation around electrical wires, to speed nerve signals and stop them leaking away. In multiple sclerosis the sheaths become damaged, hardened and scarred, or sclerosed.

In multiple sclerosis, nerve cells and the myelin coverings of their thin, delicate axons (shown here in mauve) are mistakenly attacked by the body's own defence cells (yellow).

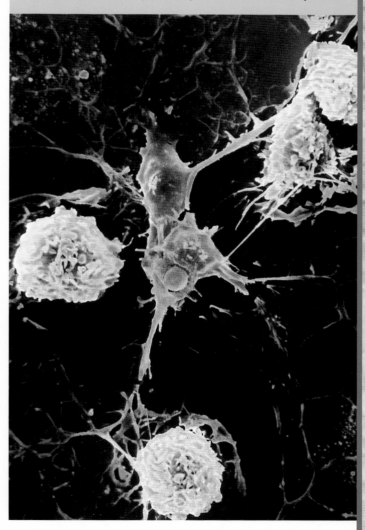

weblinks

To find out more about nerve disorders, go to:
www.waylinks.co.uk/series/ourbodies/brainandnervous

REFLEX ACTIONS

NO NEED FOR THE BRAIN

The brain controls most of the body's movements – but not all of them. In some situations, a part of the body makes a movement automatically, without the brain thinking about it or making a decision. These rapid, automatic actions are known as reflexes. Examples include the knee jerk (see below), blinking when the eye's surface is touched, sneezing when the nose is irritated by dust or germs, and pulling a body part away from danger such as a sharp point or great heat.

USEFUL REFLEXES

Most reflexes are rapid reactions to help the body keep its balance and posture, or to protect itself and avoid danger, even when the brain is busy concentrating on other thoughts. The knee-jerk reflex may happen when a person stands up for a long time. Gradually the knees may sag and bend slightly. This sets off the reflex, which jerks the knee to make the leg straight and support the body again.

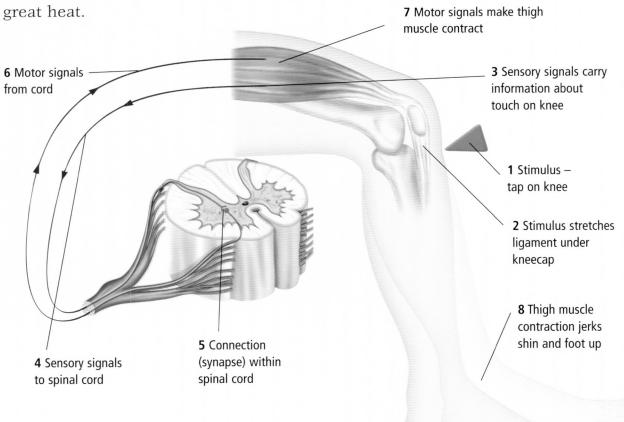

7 Motor signals make thigh muscle contract

6 Motor signals from cord

3 Sensory signals carry information about touch on knee

1 Stimulus – tap on knee

2 Stimulus stretches ligament under kneecap

8 Thigh muscle contraction jerks shin and foot up

4 Sensory signals to spinal cord

5 Connection (synapse) within spinal cord

In some fast 'reflex' actions, such as when a goalkeeper saves a ball, a person cannot recall making the decision to carry out the action. It all happens too rapidly and automatically.

HOW A REFLEX WORKS

A typical reflex starts when the body senses a sudden change which could be harmful. For example, the skin of the fingers might suddenly feel great heat, when the person's eyes and attention are directed elsewhere. Warning nerve signals flash along the nerve to the spinal cord, at a speed of 100 metres per second or more. Inside the cord, these sensory nerve signals pass directly to motor nerve cells. They immediately send signals out along their nerve fibre to nearby muscles, making them contract to carry out the movement. A split second later more signals pass up the spinal cord to the brain. The brain becomes aware of what is happening, but cannot stop the reflex.

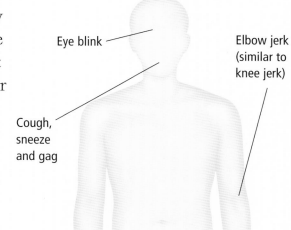

Eye blink

Elbow jerk (similar to knee jerk)

Cough, sneeze and gag

Withdrawal on feeling pain

Knee jerk

Toe curl (when sole of foot is stroked)

The body has many types of reflexes. In withdrawal, any part that senses pain is pulled away.

weblinks
To find out more about reflex actions, go to:
www.waylinks.co.uk/series/ourbodies/brainandnervous

Try this!

To test the knee-jerk reflex, sit on a chair with legs crossed, one knee under the crook of the other. Ask a friend to gently tap the uppermost leg, just below the kneecap, with a narrow item like the edge of a book. The leg 'kicks' from the knee down as the reflex action makes the muscles contract.

When we are not aware

The autonomic nervous system is made up of various parts within the brain, spinal cord and peripheral nerves. It works as part of the overall nervous system, but in ways we rarely realize. Most of its activities are subconscious – that is, they happen without our awareness. They occur automatically, without any need for us to think about them or make decisions.

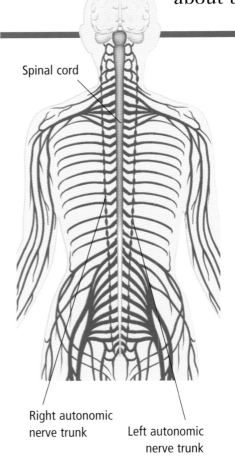

Spinal cord

Right autonomic nerve trunk

Left autonomic nerve trunk

The autonomic nervous system uses many of the same parts as the other nerve systems. Two of its major parts are the autonomic nerve trunks, chains of nerves running along each side of the spinal cord.

STEADY STATE

The autonomic nervous system deals mainly with conditions and processes inside the body. These include body temperature, heart rate, blood pressure, digestion, breathing, and making energy available for the huge variety of life processes. The autonomic system monitors all of these and more. It sends out nerve signals to adjust processes and keep conditions within the body the same, or constant, so that all body parts can work most effectively. Keeping conditions constant and stable like this, in 'steady state', is known as homeostasis.

ANIMAL VERSUS HUMAN

Antelopes graze peacefully but, if they sense danger, they race away at high speed. The autonomic nervous system makes their heart rate and breathing speed up, preparing their muscles for action in less than a second. The same happens in the human body when danger appears, but it takes a few seconds longer. It is called the 'fight or flight' reaction.

A gazelle is ready to flee from danger in a split second.

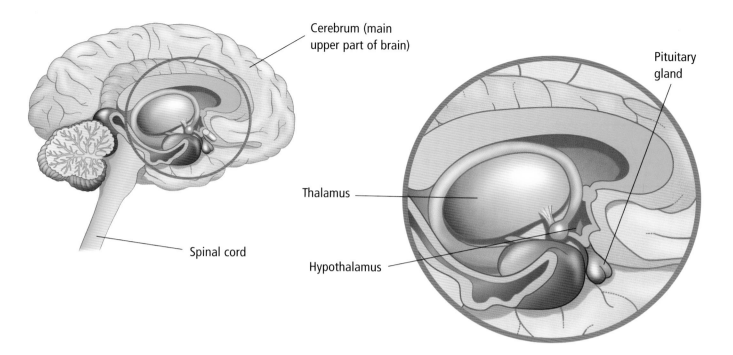

Cerebrum (main upper part of brain)

Spinal cord

Pituitary gland

Thalamus

Hypothalamus

FAST AND SLOW

The central controller of the autonomic nervous system is a small part of the brain called the hypothalamus (see pages 38–39). This sends out two sets of nerve signals, along two sets of nerve pathways, but mostly to the same body parts. One set of nerve pathways is called sympathetic, the other is parasympathetic. Sympathetic nerve messages make body parts increase their activity and work faster. For example, heart rate quickens and breathing deepens. Parasympathetic messages do the opposite. They make the parts decrease their activity and work slower. Using this double-action control, 'faster' or 'slower', the autonomic nervous system keeps the body working well inside, so the brain has time for more interesting thoughts.

When we become excited or frightened (or both), the hypothalamus makes many body parts speed up.

21

CRANIAL NERVES

Direct to the brain

Some of the body's nerves join directly to the brain, rather than the spinal cord. These are called cranial nerves and there are 12 pairs, left and right in each pair. Some are sensory nerves and bring signals from the main sense organs – the eyes, ears, nose, tongue, and the skin of the head. Others are motor nerves and carry signals to the muscles of the face, head and neck, for making movements such as chewing, swallowing, speaking and facial expressions.

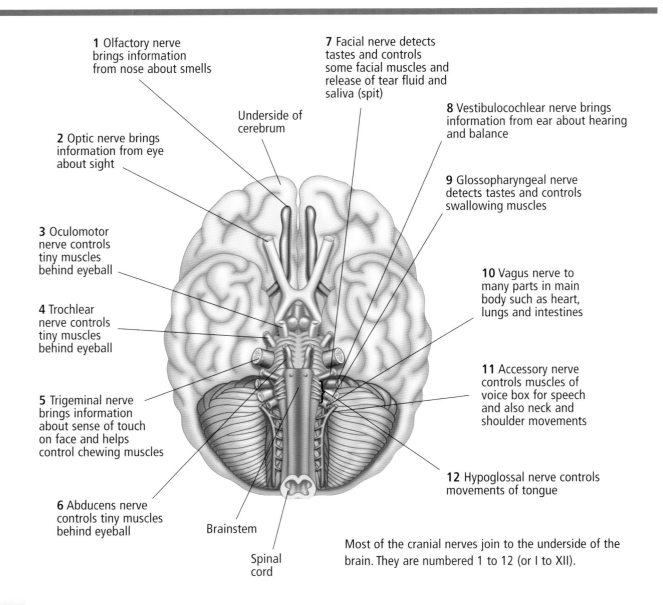

1 Olfactory nerve brings information from nose about smells

2 Optic nerve brings information from eye about sight

3 Oculomotor nerve controls tiny muscles behind eyeball

4 Trochlear nerve controls tiny muscles behind eyeball

5 Trigeminal nerve brings information about sense of touch on face and helps control chewing muscles

6 Abducens nerve controls tiny muscles behind eyeball

Underside of cerebrum

Brainstem

Spinal cord

7 Facial nerve detects tastes and controls some facial muscles and release of tear fluid and saliva (spit)

8 Vestibulocochlear nerve brings information from ear about hearing and balance

9 Glossopharyngeal nerve detects tastes and controls swallowing muscles

10 Vagus nerve to many parts in main body such as heart, lungs and intestines

11 Accessory nerve controls muscles of voice box for speech and also neck and shoulder movements

12 Hypoglossal nerve controls movements of tongue

Most of the cranial nerves join to the underside of the brain. They are numbered 1 to 12 (or I to XII).

MIXED NERVES

Some cranial nerves are 'mixed'. This means they carry both sensory and motor signals. An example is the trigeminal nerve (cranial nerve number 5), with several branches around the side of the head. It brings sensory information to the brain about touch on the eye, eyelid, the skin of the forehead and cheek, and inside the mouth including the gums. Its motor signals go to the muscles on the side of the head which work the jaws, for biting and chewing. The longest cranial nerve is the vagus (number 10), which is also mixed. It branches down through the neck to the lungs, heart, stomach and other parts in the main body.

MAIN SENSES

Ten pairs of cranial nerves join to the lower part of the brain, which is known as the brainstem. Two pairs link to the upper part of the brain, the cerebrum. These are the olfactory and optic nerves (cranial nerves numbers 1 and 2). They are both sensory, bringing vital information to the brain about what the nose smells and what the eyes see.

MICRO-BODY

The trigeminal nerve (number 5) is one of the main cranial nerves bringing nerve signals about the sense of touch on the face. Its branches extend around the eyes and also down to the cheeks, chin and jaws.

This combined medical scan shows the branches of several cranial nerves spreading out from the brainstem (arrowed).

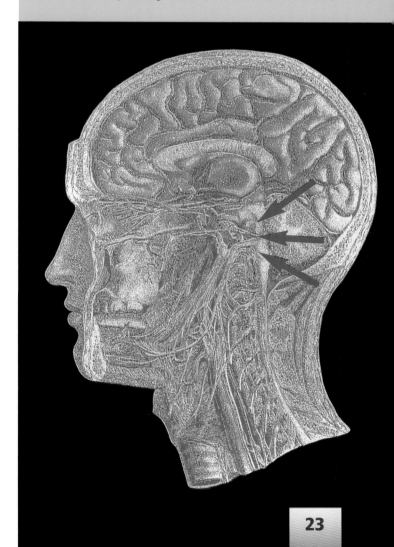

Try this!

Look at your face in a mirror. Turn your head but keep your gaze straight ahead. As your face turns to one side, your eyes swivel to the other, so you keep looking forwards. Three cranial nerves (numbers 3, 4 and 6) control the tiny muscles behind the eye that move the eyeball.

AROUND THE BRAIN

Three layers

The brain has three sheet-like layers or membranes around it, between the outside of the brain and the inside of the skull. These layers are called the dura mater (on the outside next to the skull), the arachnoid, and the pia mater (on the inside, next to the brain). Together they are known as the meninges.

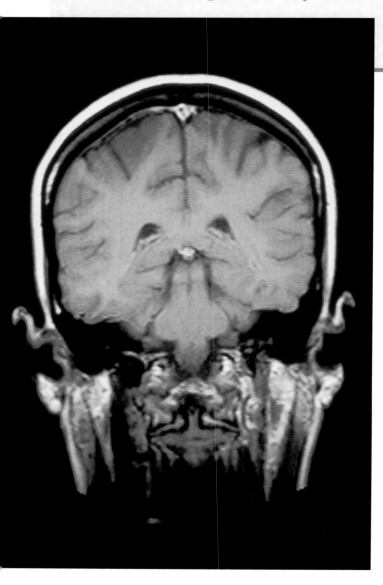

The cerebrospinal fluid shows up on a scan as a dark 'gap' around the outside of the brain.

SOFT CUSHION

The arachnoid contains many blood vessels. Also, between it and the pia mater, there is a layer of special liquid, cerebrospinal fluid. The meninges and fluid form a soft, cushion-like surrounding for the brain, so it does not bang against the inside of the skull when the head is moved suddenly or knocked. The three meninges, and the fluid between the inner two, extend all around the brain, and also downwards and around the whole length of the spinal cord. They protect and cushion the cord, too.

Top Tips

The brain has several layers of protection – meninges and fluid, skull bone, skin of the scalp, and in many people, hair too. However in some situations, like construction sites, or playing certain sports, this may not be enough. A hard-hat or helmet is needed to shield against knocks and bumps.

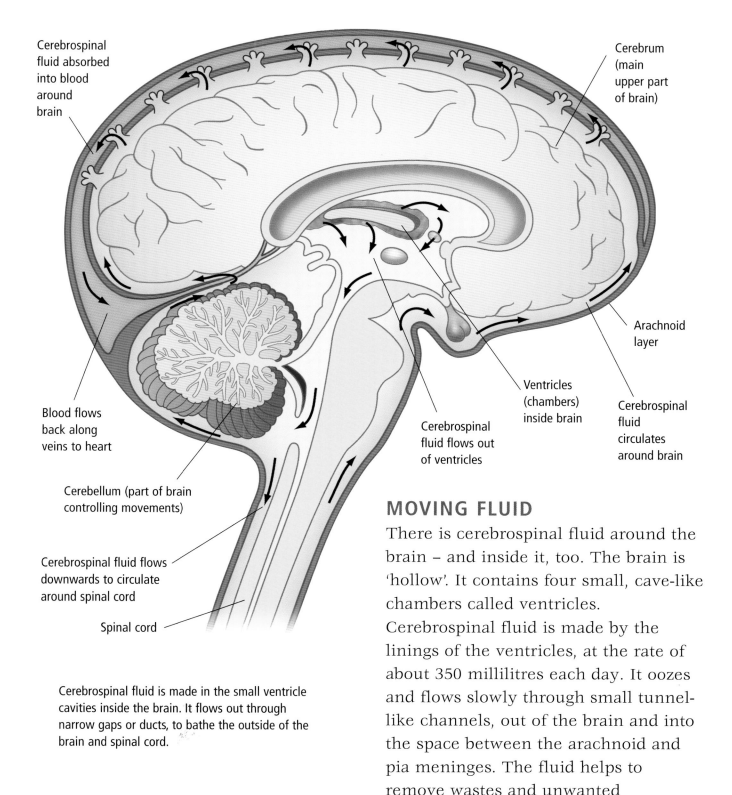

Cerebrospinal fluid absorbed into blood around brain

Cerebrum (main upper part of brain)

Blood flows back along veins to heart

Cerebellum (part of brain controlling movements)

Cerebrospinal fluid flows downwards to circulate around spinal cord

Spinal cord

Cerebrospinal fluid flows out of ventricles

Ventricles (chambers) inside brain

Arachnoid layer

Cerebrospinal fluid circulates around brain

Cerebrospinal fluid is made in the small ventricle cavities inside the brain. It flows out through narrow gaps or ducts, to bathe the outside of the brain and spinal cord.

weblinks

To find out more about the brain, go to:
www.waylinks.co.uk/series/ourbodies/brainandnervous

MOVING FLUID

There is cerebrospinal fluid around the brain – and inside it, too. The brain is 'hollow'. It contains four small, cave-like chambers called ventricles. Cerebrospinal fluid is made by the linings of the ventricles, at the rate of about 350 millilitres each day. It oozes and flows slowly through small tunnel-like channels, out of the brain and into the space between the arachnoid and pia meninges. The fluid helps to remove wastes and unwanted substances, and is absorbed at the same rate it is made, by the blood vessels in the arachnoid layer.

BRAIN AND NERVE INJURIES

Causes of injury

The brain and spinal cord are so vital that if they suffer injury, the person's life may be in danger. Knocks, blows or wounds to the head, neck, chest and back are the most common causes of brain or cord injury. They occur most often in road accidents and falls. Other causes include bullets from guns, knife wounds, collisions during sports, and diving into water which is too shallow.

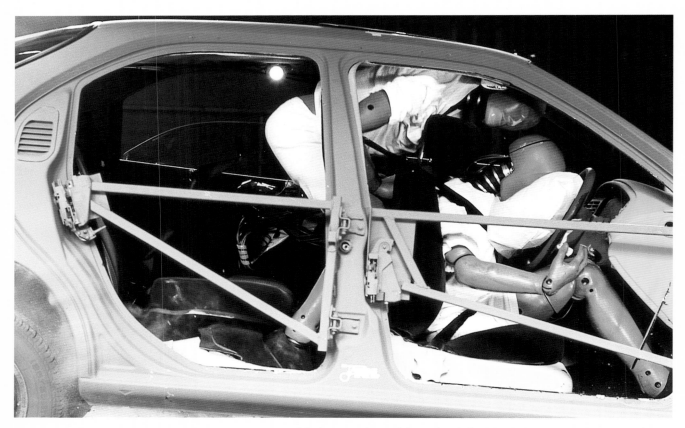

Modern cars have airbags that inflate in an emergency, to prevent the head smashing forwards and damaging the face and brain.

EFFECTS OF INJURY

Sometimes a brain or spinal cord injury is minor. However almost any kind of damage to the nervous system takes a long time to heal, usually weeks or months. In more serious cases the person is disabled or affected for years, even for life. Damage to the lower spinal cord affects the lower body and legs, causing varying amounts of numbness, paralysis, and perhaps loss of control of the bladder and bowels. Damage to the upper spinal cord, in the neck, affects the arms as well. It may even cause problems with breathing which can threaten life.

KNOCK-OUT

A blow to the head may cause concussion – brief loss of consciousness, when the person 'blacks out' or is 'knocked out'. In some cases the person may seem to recover, apart from a sore head. But there might be underlying damage such as bleeding into or around the brain, called a haemorrhage. Anyone who is knocked out, even for a few seconds, should consult medical staff for a check-up and perhaps tests like a scan or X-ray.

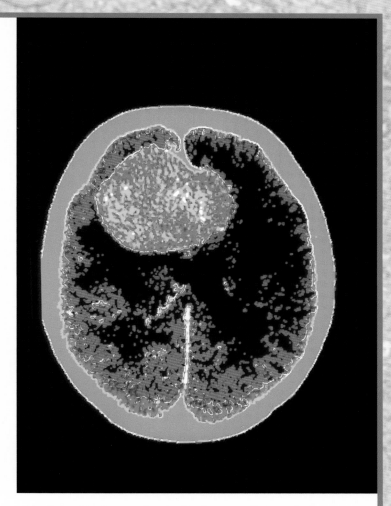

A horizontal brain scan (level with the ground) through the upper part of the head shows the brain's main upper part, the cerebrum. A large area of blood (green and blue) has haemorrhaged or leaked into and over it.

Top Tips

Everyone who rides a bicycle thinks that a fall or crash will not happen – until it does. It may not be the rider's fault, but it is the rider's head and brain which are at risk. This is why it is so important to wear hard or padded cycle helmets. In most cycle sports, they must be worn as part of the regular rules.

THE BRAINSTEM

The 'stalk' of the brain

Most of the brain is made of the large, bulging, wrinkled part at the top, known as the cerebrum. Below this, the brain becomes narrower as it tapers downwards to join the spinal cord. This lowest part of the brain, which is like a stalk or the trunk of a tree, is called the brainstem.

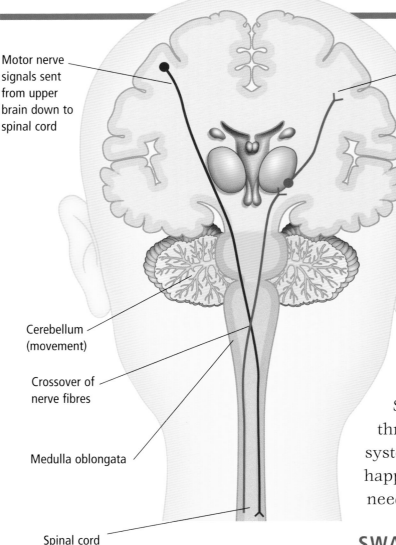

Motor nerve signals sent from upper brain down to spinal cord

Sensory nerve signals from skin on right side of body arrive in upper left side of brain

Cerebellum (movement)

Crossover of nerve fibres

Medulla oblongata

Spinal cord

Nerve fibres from the body change sides as they pass through the medulla of the lower brain.

VITAL FOR LIFE

The brainstem is mainly involved in basic life processes. Different small areas inside it, known as centres, control body activities which are essential for life. These include heart rate, breathing, digestion, getting rid of wastes, blood pressure and body temperature. Such processes are controlled through the autonomic nervous system (see pages 20–21). They happen automatically, without the need to think about them.

SWAPPED OVER

The lowest part of the brainstem, just above the spinal cord, is the medulla oblongata. It is slightly wider and shorter than a thumb. Thousands of nerve fibres pass through it, between the spinal cord below and the higher 'thinking' parts of the brain above. However, on their way through the medulla, the nerve fibres from the left side of the spinal cord pass over to the right side. Similarly the right-side fibres cross to the left. This means the right side of the brain receives messages from, and sends message to, the left side of the body. In the same way, the brain's left side receives sensations from, and controls muscles in, the body's right side.

Nerve signals for moving the left arm to catch a ball, and feeling the ball arrive, happen in the right side of the brain.

ANIMAL VERSUS HUMAN

The octopus has a very big brain for its body size. However the brain is not in the top of its head, as in most animals. It's in the lower part of its body, and it has a hole in the middle – for the octopus's gullet (food pipe)!

The octopus's brain is below its eyes, not above.

Go-betweens

In the middle of the brain are parts called the thalamus and basal ganglia. They are between the 'automatic' or 'non-thinking' parts of the brain below, and the 'thinking' parts above. They have various complicated tasks in the overall workings of the brain.

The middle parts of the brain have complex shapes and functions. The hippocampus is involved in memory and the caudate and lentiform nuclei are parts of the basal ganglia (see opposite).

Caudate nucleus

Hippocampus

Thalamus

Medulla

Spinal cord

Lentiform nucleus

Amygdala

FRONT VIEW

THE THALAMUS

The thalamus consists of two egg-shaped parts which have nerve links with many other areas of the brain. It is sometimes compared to a main exchange in the telephone system. It receives nerve messages from certain parts of the brain, and sends them on, or relays them, to other parts. For example, the thalamus relays sensory nerve signals from the eyes, ears and other sense organs (apart from the nose), to higher brain parts. It also sorts out and directs motor nerve signals heading out to control muscles and movements. And the thalamus is involved in the brain's levels of awareness – from being fully awake and alert, to relaxed and resting, feeling tired and drowsy, and falling into a deep sleep.

FAMILIAR MOVEMENTS

Around the thalamus are several brain parts which make up the basal ganglia. Early in life, a young child learns many basic movements, like chewing, swallowing, and the leg and arm actions of walking. These become so familiar and easy that we do them 'almost without thinking'. The basal ganglia are important in controlling and carrying out these movements.

---

weblinks

To find out more about how the brain works, go to:
www.waylinks.co.uk/series/ourbodies/brainandnervous

Try this!

Find a very quiet place to sit in safety for a few minutes. It may seem silent – but is it? Listen hard to every tiny sound. Are there noises which you did not realize at first, like whirring machinery, distant traffic or the wind? Your ears always receive these. But parts of the brain such as the thalamus are always monitoring them. If the sounds do not seem important, they are not brought into your full awareness, and your mind 'ignores' them.

MICRO-BODY

In the condition known as Parkinson's disease, movements become weak and trembling due to problems in the basal ganglia.

In Parkinson's disease the microscopic nerve cells of the substantia nigra, which is in the lowermost area of the basal ganglia, fail to work properly due to a lack of neurotransmitter chemicals.

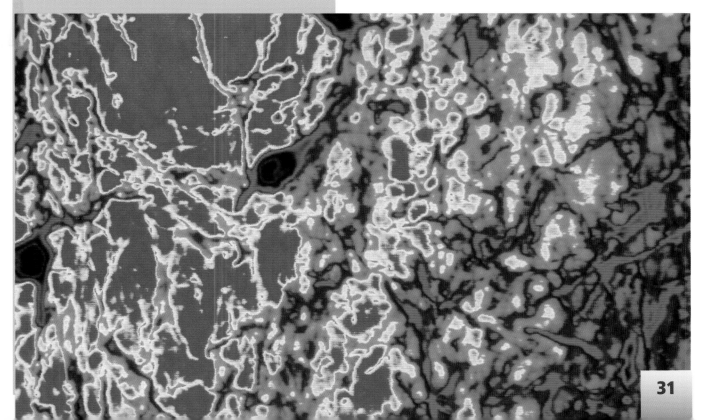

THE CEREBELLUM AND MOVEMENT

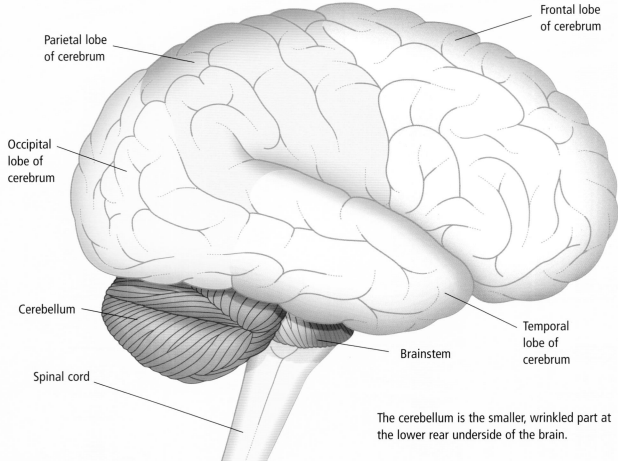

Parietal lobe
of cerebrum

Frontal lobe
of cerebrum

Occipital
lobe of
cerebrum

Cerebellum

Temporal
lobe of
cerebrum

Brainstem

Spinal cord

The cerebellum is the smaller, wrinkled part at
the lower rear underside of the brain.

MUSCLE CONTROL

When we decide to make a movement, the nerve signals that represent this thought are in the uppermost domed part of the brain, the cerebrum. This part sends more signals along nerve fibres, through the middle of the brain, and down to the round, wrinkled part at the lower rear. This is called the cerebellum and it makes up about one-tenth of the brain's total size. The cerebellum's main tasks are to control the individual muscles which move the body.

SMOOTHER AND MORE SKILFUL

Even a simple movement like raising the arm uses more than 20 muscles. The nerve signals from the cerebrum to the cerebellum are not very detailed—for example, giving the general instruction, "lift the arm." The cerebellum then fills in the details and sends out signals to the individual muscles that are needed for that movement. It controls the muscles in groups or teams, so that they work together in a precise and coordinated way. This means we can learn to make our movements smoother and more skilled—whether it's lifting heavy weights, or adding tiny details to a drawing.

Feedback

As a movement happens, the cerebellum receives incoming nerve messages from movement sensors in the muscles and joints. These tell it how fast the movement is occurring and how far the body parts have changed position, many times each second. Using this feedback the cerebellum can then adjust its outgoing signals to the muscles, controlling how much they pull or contract, and how fast they work, so the action happens in a smooth and coordinated way.

Try this!

With pen and paper, close your eyes, then write a common saying like "The cat sat on the mat." Now look. How neat are the words? The cerebellum plays a large part in familiar, practiced, delicate actions like writing. However, it is helpful to see the words as they are written. Then we can make adjustments like keeping the line straight and the letters the same size.

This windsurfer is relying greatly on the brain's cerebellum to control the details of muscle movements, while the thinking parts of the brain concentrate on more major decisions.

THE CORTEX AND THINKING

Grey matter

The biggest, most bulging, most wrinkled part of the brain is the cerebrum. It forms more than nine-tenths of the brain's total volume, and it covers the other, smaller parts beneath it. The cerebrum has an outer grey layer known as the cerebral cortex. This is similar to the 'grey matter' inside the spinal cord and covering the cerebellum. It is made of billions and billions of nerve cell bodies, with trillions and trillions of dendrite connections. Under the grey cerebral cortex are layers of much paler 'white matter'. These are mainly nerve fibres, linking the nerve cells of the cortex with other parts of the brain below.

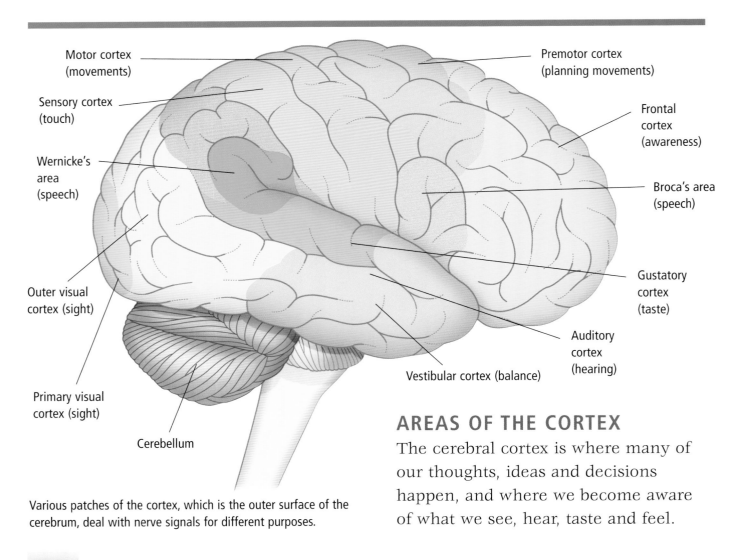

Motor cortex (movements)
Premotor cortex (planning movements)
Sensory cortex (touch)
Frontal cortex (awareness)
Wernicke's area (speech)
Broca's area (speech)
Outer visual cortex (sight)
Gustatory cortex (taste)
Primary visual cortex (sight)
Auditory cortex (hearing)
Cerebellum
Vestibular cortex (balance)

Various patches of the cortex, which is the outer surface of the cerebrum, deal with nerve signals for different purposes.

AREAS OF THE CORTEX

The cerebral cortex is where many of our thoughts, ideas and decisions happen, and where we become aware of what we see, hear, taste and feel.

It looks much the same all over. But areas or patches of it are specialized for dealing with nerve signals coming from, or going to, different body parts. For example, around the lower rear of the cerebrum is the visual cortex. This receives and sorts nerve messages from the eyes, and compares them with information already in the brain, about shapes and colours and patterns. This is how we can make sense of what we see and recognize scenes and objects. There are similar areas of cortex for hearing, touch, taste, balance, understanding speech and writing, speaking words, and planning and making movements (motor cortex).

The nerve cell bodies in the cortex are shown as dark spots, and the dendrites as thin lines, in this micro-view.

Try this!

Sit in front of a sheet of card, and draw a dot somewhere on it. Close your eyes, and after a few seconds, try to touch the dot with your finger. You can remember a picture of the card in your 'mind's eye', and move your hand to reach it (or quite near). This type of memory, called visual-spatial awareness, is based in the frontal cortex (see opposite).

MICRO-BODY

The cortex of the cerebrum contains billions of nerve cell bodies, with their dendrites linking to each other to form an incredibly complex network. This is where most general thinking or mental processes happen.

A BRAIN OF TWO HALVES

Hemispheres

The main bulging part of the **brain,** the cerebrum, has a rounded shape like a wrinkled soccer ball. But there is an extra-deep groove from front to back that almost divides the cerebrum into two halves. These halves are called the left and right cerebral hemispheres. At the base of the split is a connecting strap between the two halves, called the corpus callosum. This contains more than 100 million **nerve** fibers. They carry nerve signals between the left and right halves, so information can be sent back and forth.

When a person plays music with great feeling, the right side of the brain tends to be in charge, or dominant, over the left side.

Two halves make a whole

The two cerebral hemispheres appear similar. But they have slightly different jobs. Usually, one is "dominant," and takes charge over the other. For example, areas called speech centers in each hemisphere deal with the process of choosing words, putting them into a sensible order, and speaking them out loud. In most people, by the age of 8–10 years, the left speech center becomes dominant and takes charge, while the right one is quiet or "dormant."

Left and right

There are other differences in the ways that the left and right sides work. In general, the left side has more to do with words and language, numbers and math, and solving problems in a step-by-step way. The right side tends to deal more with intuition or "jumping" to answers, and awareness of shapes, patterns, colors, and musical sounds. Of course, in daily life, both halves of the brain work closely together.

ANIMAL VERSUS HUMAN

About one person in ten prefers to use the left hand for holding, writing, and similar actions, while the rest prefer the right hand. Animals like chimpanzees also prefer to use one hand rather than the other, for detailed tasks. Even snails can be "left-handed" or "right-handed." Seen from above, a left-handed snail shell twists to the left (counter-clockwise) while others swirl to the right.

FEELINGS AND EMOTIONS

Where is 'the mind'?

There is no single place in the brain which can be called 'the mind', where all thoughts, ideas and memories happen. Different parts of the brain work together in a very complicated way. This includes the way that people experience strong feelings and powerful emotions, such as fear, anger, rage, pain, pleasure and love. Many parts of the cerebral cortex are involved in these feelings. Millions of nerve messages pass between them, and are sent out to other brain parts, especially the thalamus, the cerebellum and the hypothalamus.

EMOTIONS AND BEHAVIOUR

Sometimes feelings and emotions are so strong, a person seems overwhelmed by them and unable to think clearly or sensibly. This type of behaviour especially involves the hypothalamus, a small part at the lower front of the brain. It receives nerve messages from the cerebral cortex and other brain areas, and sends out its own signals through the autonomic nervous system (see pages 20–21) to many body parts. This causes reactions which accompany powerful emotions,

Bad news can cause such powerful emotions that they take over the sensible, rational, 'thinking' functions of the brain.

like quickened heart rate, panting (fast, shallow breathing), blushing of the skin, sweaty or clammy hands and face, dry mouth, and 'butterflies' or 'flutterings' in the stomach and digestive system.

HOT AND THIRSTY

The hypothalamus performs many other vital jobs. It has a 'temperature centre' which helps to monitor and adjust body temperature, to keep this within a very narrow range, usually 37 degrees Celsius. It also has a 'thirst centre' which checks the amount of water in the blood. This, in turn, shows the amount of water in the body. If there is too little, the hypothalamus makes us feel thirsty.

Try this!

Try to remember an event which was very pleasing, satisfying or pleasurable. Do you get a 'warm glow' inside, and perhaps a prickly or tingling sensation in the skin? This is the hypothalamus at work, making the body react to feelings of pleasure in the brain – even from memories.

The hypothalamus is hardly larger than the tip of a little finger. Yet it has very important roles in many vital brain activities, including links with the body's second control system, the hormonal system, through the pituitary gland just below it.

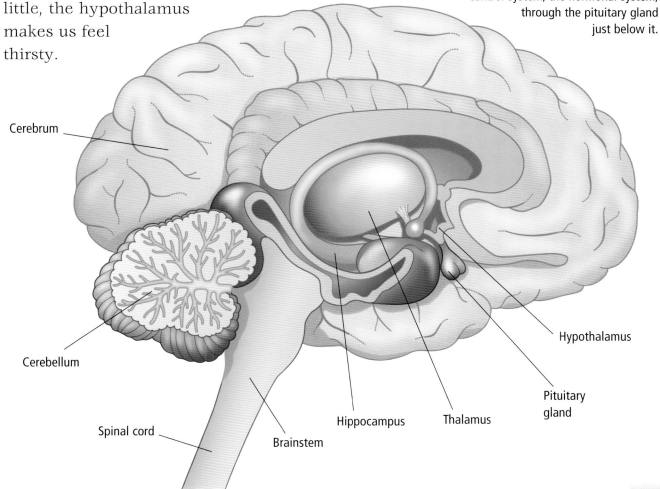

Cerebrum

Cerebellum

Spinal cord

Brainstem

Hippocampus

Thalamus

Hypothalamus

Pituitary gland

LEARNING

Learning all the time

How much will you learn today? We learn at school, but we also learn in other ways during everyday life, often without realizing it. We learn how to behave in certain situations, our likes and dislikes, and information about our family and friends. Whatever we learn is stored as memories in the **brain,** so we can recall or remember them later.

Parts involved in memory

Like other types of thinking and behaving, there does not appear to be a single place in the brain where all memories are stored. Memories are a result of many parts working together. These parts include various areas of the cerebral cortex, especially toward the front side of the brain (known as the prefrontal cortex); the thalamus; and also parts at the center of the cerebrum, the amygdala and hippocampus.

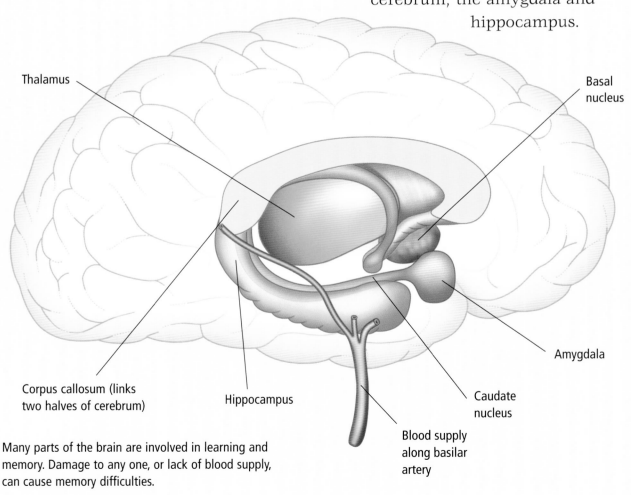

Thalamus

Basal nucleus

Corpus callosum (links two halves of cerebrum)

Hippocampus

Caudate nucleus

Amygdala

Blood supply along basilar artery

Many parts of the brain are involved in learning and memory. Damage to any one, or lack of blood supply, can cause memory difficulties.

Multiple memories

It is likely that different parts or sections of what seem like one memory are stored in different parts of the brain. For example, imagine the memory of an exciting event like a rollercoaster ride. What you can recall of the sounds of the ride may come from one part of the brain, while you remember the sights in another, and the memory of your bodily feelings is in yet another place. These "pieces of memories" probably exist as sets of connections or pathways for **nerve** signals between nerve **cells**.

ANIMAL VERSUS HUMAN

Legend has it that elephants have very long memories. Modern science shows that these age-old beliefs are true. The chief of the herd is an older female elephant, the matriarch. Studies show that she learns where there are fresh areas of plant growth to return to each year, and remembers waterholes for drinking. She builds up these memories over her lifetime, which may be more than 70 years.

BRAIN DISORDERS

Physical and mental

The brain is so important and complicated, that if it goes wrong, it can have many effects on the body. Some brain disorders are physical, which means they have a clear cause which can be detected by medical examination, X-rays, scans, or tests on brain chemicals like neurotransmitters. Other problems, including certain mental or behavioural disorders, have causes which are less easy to identify. But they are just as real for the sufferer. They are based in the mind and affect moods and emotions, and the way people think, talk, react and cope with stress.

HEADACHE

Headaches are common, yet the brain itself cannot detect pain. It does not have suitable nerve sensors. The aching sensations usually come from around the brain, in the meninges (coverings), blood vessels and other surrounding parts. Also a headache is not really a single disorder. It is a part or symptom of an underlying problem, which may range from tiredness and lack of sleep, to worry and stress, a bang on the head, or rarely, a growth or tumour in the brain.

Headaches often occur when a person is under stress, working long hours and worrying about career or home life.

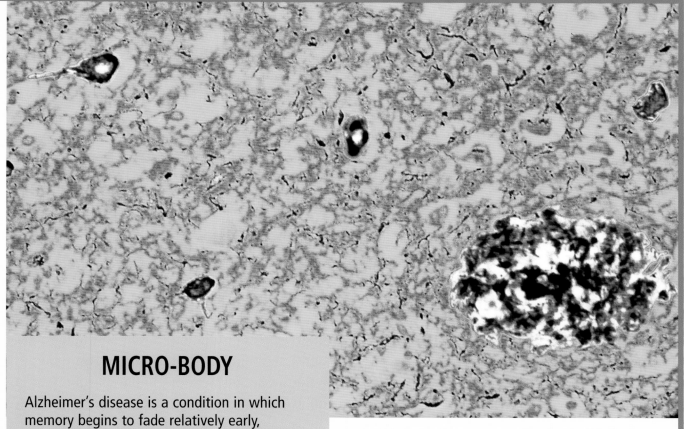

MICRO-BODY

Alzheimer's disease is a condition in which memory begins to fade relatively early, compared to the normal process of ageing. The person may even forget family and friends.

In Alzheimer's disease, nerve cells in parts of the brain develop 'tangles' (blue) as their dendrites and fibres are damaged and lose their connections.

STROKE AND EPILEPSY

In a stroke, a blood vessel supplying the brain gets blocked. Blood cannot bring vital oxygen and nutrients, so parts of the brain suffer damage. Signs of a stroke include numbness and paralysis, perhaps on one side of the body, loss of speech, and possibly collapse. In the group of conditions known as epilepsy, nerve signals pass through the brain in a random, disorganized way. This may cause jerky movements known as a seizure or convulsions, and possibly unconsciousness.

BRAIN WAVES

The medical EEG (electroencephalo-graph) machine detects the tiny electrical pulses of nerve signals in the brain, through pads on the head. It shows these signals as waves and spikes on screen or paper. EEGs help to identify various brain disorders so that treatment is more successful.

weblinks

To find out more about brain disorders, go to:
www.waylinks.co.uk/series/ourbodies/brainandnervous

SLEEP AND DREAMS

Why do we sleep?

The sleeping **brain** is very busy, as shown by its EEG waves. But exactly what it does at this time is still partly a mystery. Recent studies show that one of the brain's tasks may be "memory-sorting." It works through its stores of memories, keeps some that are important, and throws away or forgets others.

Falling asleep

As a person falls into deep sleep, the body slows down, muscles relax, and heart rate and breathing decrease. Some processes, such as digestion and formation of urine (liquid waste) in the kidneys, also become slower. But others, like repair of wounds or damage, are faster.

REM sleep

After about one hour of deep sleep, heart rate and breathing quicken, muscles twitch, and the eyes move rapidly back and forth, even though the eyelids are closed. This is called REM (rapid eye movement) sleep, and it is when dreams occur. A person who wakes up at this time usually remembers the dream. On most nights, we pass through this first REM sleep and sink into deep sleep for another hour or so, then repeat more cycles of REM and deep sleep until morning.

Sleep varies from deep (non-REM) to shallow (REM) in stages through the night, with different EEG traces for each level (below).

Falling asleep

Waking up

REM sleep

A W A K E
A S L E E P

Shallowest sleep (stages 1 and 2)

Fairly deep sleep (stage 3)

Deep sleep gradually gets shallower towards morning

Deep sleep (stage 4)

| 1 Hour | 2 Hours | 3 Hours | 4 Hours | 5 Hours | 6 Hours | 7 Hours | 8 Hours |

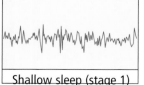
Shallow sleep (stage 1)

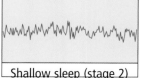
Shallow sleep (stage 2)

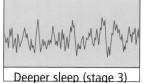
Deeper sleep (stage 3)

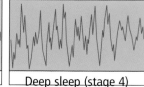
Deep sleep (stage 4)

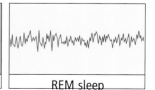
REM sleep

The need for sleep

Whatever the brain does during sleep, it seems to be important, since we need enough regular sleep to stay healthy. Lack of sleep causes headaches, confusion, dizziness, poor concentration, bad temper, and loss of memory. It also makes the body more at risk from disease and infections. Sleep, like many functions of the brain and **nerves,** is complicated and fascinating. Indeed the brain is not only the control center of the body and the site of the mind—it is the only object that can find out more about itself.

Research continues into the amazingly complex workings of the brain. Even "simple" sleep is still poorly understood.

Top Tips

Some people have trouble falling asleep, or wake up too early and cannot go back to sleep. There are many pieces of advice to help them:

Adjust the bed and its covers for comfort, so it is not too warm or cold.

Think of pleasant events such as vacations.

Relax each muscle one at a time, and breathe slowly.

Put aside cares and worries until the next day, when something can be done about them.

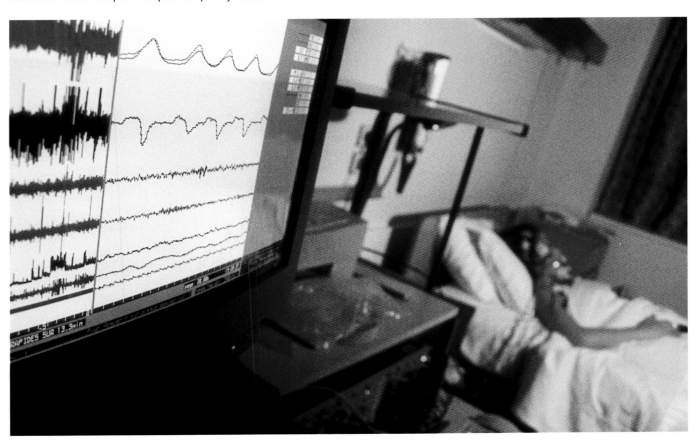

GLOSSARY

autonomic nervous system Parts of the nervous system that work automatically, without us having to think about them or control them, to keep conditions inside the body constant, and to control vital bodily processes like breathing and heart rate.

axon The long, thin part of a nerve cell, also called a nerve fibre, which carries nerve signals away from the cell body and passes them on to other nerve cells.

brain An incredibly complex part of the body, in the upper part of the head, made of billions of nerve cells and nerve fibres. The brain receives information from the senses, controls the body's movements, and is the site of thoughts, memories, conscious awareness and the mind.

cell A single unit or 'building block' of life – the human body is made of billions of cells of many different kinds.

cell body The main part of a microscopic cell, which is usually rounded and contains tiny parts such as the cell's nucleus or control centre.

central nervous system The brain and spinal cord.

cranium The 'brain-case' – the curved, dome-shaped bones of the upper skull which surround and protect the brain.

dendrites Short, thin, branching parts of a nerve cell, which receive nerve signals from other nerve cells and carry them towards the cell body.

epineurium The covering or sheath around a nerve.

fascicle A group of nerve fibres within a nerve, like a bundle or wires within an electrical cable.

ganglion A lump-like part of a nerve which contains a group or gathering of the cell bodies from nerve cells.

impulse A tiny surge or pulse of electricity that passes along a nerve, also called a nerve signal or nerve message.

motor In the body, to do with movements or motions, such as motor nerves which carry motor nerve signals to the muscles to control their movements.

myelin sheath The covering of certain nerve fibres (axons), made of a sheet of the fatty substance myelin wrapped round and round the fibre, like a roll of cooking foil.

nerves Long, thin, string-like parts inside the body, which carry information in the form of nerve impulses or signals.

neurotoxins Poisonous substances which have a harmful effect on the body by damaging nerves or stopping them working properly.

olfactory To do with the sense of smell.

optic To do with the sense of sight (vision).

parasympathetic Parts of the autonomic nervous system (see above) which make the body work more slowly, for example, by decreasing the rate at which the heart beats and the lungs breathe.

peripheral nervous system The network of nerves that branch out to all body parts from the brain and spinal cord, but not including the brain and spinal cord.

reflex A quick automatic reaction by the body, to a sudden change or situation which could be harmful, such as blinking the eyes if something comes near them.

sciatic nerve The thickest peripheral nerve in the body, which runs from the hip down through the thigh to the knee.

sclerosed Hardened, stiffened and toughened.

sensory In the body, to do with parts that detect what happens in the surroundings, such as the eyes which sense light, and the sensory nerves which carry sensory nerve signals to the brain.

spinal cord The body's main nerve, extending from the base of the brain down through the spinal column of backbones to the waist.

subconscious Happening in the brain, but without the mind being aware of it during conscious thoughts.

sympathetic Parts of the autonomic nervous system (see above) which make the body work faster, for example, by increasing the rate at which the heart beats and the lungs breathe.

synaptic gap The tiny gap or space in the connection or junction (synapse) between two nerve cells, where they do not quite touch, but where nerve signals can pass across in chemical form.

vertebrae The individual bones of the backbone (spinal column or vertebral column).

FURTHER INFORMATION

BOOKS

Body Focus: Brain/Spinal Cord and Nerves (Heinemann, 2004)

Body Science: Inside the Brain by Rufus Bellamy (Franklin Watts, 2004)

Brain Box: the Brain, Nervous System and Senses by Patricia Macnair (Kingfisher, 2005)

Under the Microscope: Brain by Richard Walker (Franklin Watts, 2001)

ORGANIZATIONS

National Society for Epilepsy

The NSE aims to provide information and raise awareness among people affected by epilepsy and among the general public.

Chesham Lane, Chalfont St Peter,
Bucks SL9 0RJ

Tel: 01494 601300   Helpline: 01494 601400

Epilepsy Action

The UK's largest member-led epilepsy organization, acting for the UK's estimated 440,000 people with epilepsy, as well as their friends, families, carers and health professionals.

New Anstey House, Gate Way Drive,
Yeadon, Leeds LS19 7XY
Tel: 0113 210 8800   Helpline: 0808 800 5050

The Stroke Association

Funding research into the prevention of strokes, treatment and better methods of their rehabilitation, and producing a wide selection of printed materials.

Stroke House, 240 City Road,
London EC1V 2PR
Tel: 020 7566 0300   Helpline: 0845 30 33 100

Mind

The leading mental health charity in England and Wales, working for a better life for everyone with experience of mental distress.

15–19 Broadway, London E15 4BQ
Tel: 020 8519 2122

Multiple Sclerosis International Federation

MSIF advises and supports those with MS, their families, friends and carers.

3rd Floor Skyline House, 200 Union Street,
London SE1 0LX
Tel: 020 7620 1911

Migraine Action Association

Formerly the British Migraine Association, MAA aims to bridge the gap between the migraine sufferer and the medical world by providing information on all aspects of the condition.

Unit 6, Oakley Hay Lodge Business Park,
Great Folds Road, Great Oakley,
Northants NN18 9AS
Tel: 01536 461333

INDEX